W9-CIH-229

WITHDRAWN

OSCEOLA

BY SANTANA HUNT

Gareth Stevens
PUBLISHING

Please visit our website, www.garethstevens.com. For a free color catalog of all our high-quality books, call toll free 1-800-542-2595 or fax 1-877-542-2596.

Library of Congress Cataloging-in-Publication Data

Hunt, Santana.
 Osceola / Santana Hunt.
     pages cm. — (Native American heroes)
 Includes bibliographical references and index.
 ISBN 978-1-4824-2689-2 (pbk.)
 ISBN 978-1-4824-2690-8 (6 pack)
 ISBN 978-1-4824-2691-5 (library binding)
 1. Osceola, Seminole chief, 1804-1838—Juvenile literature. 2. Seminole Indians—Biography—Juvenile literature. 3. Seminole Indians—Wars—Juvenile literature. I. Title.
 E99.S28H86 2015
 975.90049738590092—dc23
 [B]

                                        2014048107

Published in 2016 by
Gareth Stevens Publishing
111 East 14th Street, Suite 349
New York, NY 10003

Designer: Laura Bowen
Editor: Kristen Rajczak

Photo credits: Cover, p. 1 SuperStock/Getty Images; cover, pp. 1–24 (series art) Binkski/Shutterstock.com; pp. 5, 7 Hulton Archive/Getty Images; pp. 9, 13 MPI/Archive Photos/Getty Images; p. 11 Popperfoto/Getty Images; p. 15 blinkblink/Shutterstock.com; p. 17 Daderot/Wikimedia Commons; p. 19 (main) Print Collector/Hulton Archive/Getty Images; p. 19 (inset) Hugh Manatee/Wikimedia Commons; p. 21 Ruth Peterkin/Shutterstock.com.

Printed in the United States of America

CPSIA compliance information: Batch #CS15GS: For further information contact Gareth Stevens, New York, New York at 1-800-542-2595.

CONTENTS

Boldface words appear in the glossary.

Remembering Osceola

Osceola was a leader of the Seminole **tribe** during the 1830s. He was a great speaker and a brave fighter. Many remember Osceola for standing up for his people against the US government!

5

Life in the Creek Tribe

Osceola, or Billy Powell as he is sometimes known, was born in 1804. He lived in Alabama with his mother. Osceola was part of the Creek tribe because his mother was. However, his father may have been English.

7

Creek tribes in Alabama were fighting each other during 1813 and 1814. While the war went on, Osceola, his mother, and others from their tribe left for Florida. They later settled with the Seminoles, a tribe with ties to the Creeks.

Seminole village

9

Fighting in Florida

In 1817 and 1818, General Andrew Jackson led US troops against the Seminoles in Florida. The tribe was known for fighting against new white settlers. They also hid **slaves** who had escaped. Florida was owned by Spain at the time.

Andrew Jackson

11

Forced to Leave

In 1821, Florida became a US **territory**. Soon after, all Native American tribes were asked to move west. When the Indian Removal Act passed in 1830, it was clear tribes didn't have a choice. Osceola and others were angry about it.

Some Seminole chiefs signed **treaties** with the US government. They agreed to leave Florida for "Indian Territory" in modern-day Oklahoma. Osceola became a leader of those against these treaties.

UNITED STATES, 1830

Michigan Territory

New York

Pennsylvania

Maryland

Ohio

Illinois

Indiana

Virginia

Missouri
Territory

Missouri

Kentucky

North Carolina

Tennessee

Arkansas
Territory

South
Carolina

Mississippi

Alabama

Georgia

MEXICO

Atlantic
Ocean

Louisiana

Florida
Territory

Gulf of
Mexico

 tribal territory

 land granted by Indian Removal Act

Osceola Opposes

Osceola led a group of Seminoles to **defend** their land. In 1835, they killed a chief who was going to obey the treaty. They also killed a US **official**. These actions made Osceola an outlaw.

In 1837, Osceola and other Seminole leaders went to St. Augustine, Florida, to meet with US General Thomas Jesup. They wanted to make peace and arrived under a flag of **truce**. However, Osceola was taken prisoner instead!

Thomas Jesup

19

A National Hero

Osceola had become well-known for defending the Seminole tribe. When he died in prison in 1838, both his people and other Americans saw him as a hero. Today, Osceola is still honored for his bravery.

TIMELINE OF OSCEOLA'S LIFE

1804 — Osceola is born.

1813– 1814 — Osceola leaves Alabama and settles with the Seminoles.

1821 — Florida becomes a US territory.

1830 — The Indian Removal Act passes.

1835 — Osceola leads a group to oppose treaties with the US government.

1837 — Osceola is taken prisoner.

1838 — Osceola dies.

GLOSSARY

defend: to keep something safe

official: someone who works and acts for a government or group

slave: a person "owned" by another person and forced to work without pay

territory: land owned by a country

treaty: an agreement between countries or groups

tribe: a group of people who live, work, and move about together

truce: an agreement to end fighting for a period of time

FOR MORE INFORMATION

BOOKS

McGovern, Ann. *Native American Heroes: Osceola, Tecumseh & Cochise.* New York, NY: Scholastic Inc., 2013.

Sanford, William R. *Seminole Chief Osceola.* Berkeley Heights, NJ: Enslow Publishers, 2013.

WEBSITES

Native American Biographies
www.socialstudiesforkids.com/subjects/ nativeamericanbiographies.htm
Find out about other famous Native Americans in history here.

Seminole Indian Fact Sheet
www.bigorrin.org/seminole_kids.htm
Learn more about Osceola's tribe.

INDEX